Wine lover's kitchen

Wine lover's kitchen

Delicious recipes for cooking with wine

FIONA BECKETT

photography by
Mowie Kay

LONDON • NEW YORK

For Will, with love. Here's a way to use all that wine...

Senior Designer Sonya Nathoo
Editor Miriam Catley
Head of Production Patricia Harrington
Art Director Leslie Harrington
Editorial Director Julia Charles
Publisher Cindy Richards

Food stylists Rosie Reynolds, Sian Henley and Emily Kydd
Prop stylist Jennifer Kay
Indexer Vanessa Bird

First published in 2017
by Ryland Peters & Small
20–21 Jockey's Fields
London WC1R 4BW
and
341 E 116th St
New York NY 10029

www.rylandpeters.com

10 9 8 7 6 5 4 3 2 1

Some recipes in this book were previously published by Ryland Peters & Small as *Cooking with Wine* 2005

ISBN: 978-1-84975-881-9

Printed in China

A CIP record for this book is available from the British Library. US Library of Congress Cataloging-in-Publication Data has been applied for.

Notes

- Both British (Metric) and American (Imperial plus US cups) ingredients measurements are included in these recipes for your convenience, however it is important to work with one set of measurements and not alternate between the two within a recipe.
- All spoon measurements are level unless otherwise specified.
- All eggs are medium (UK) or large (US), unless specified as large, in which case US extra-large should be used. Uncooked or partially cooked eggs should not be served to the very old, frail, young children, pregnant women or those with compromised immune systems.
- When a recipe calls for the grated zest of citrus fruit, buy unwaxed fruit and wash well before using. If you can only find treated fruit, scrub well in warm soapy water before using.
- To sterilize glass storage jars, wash them in hot, soapy water and rinse in boiling water. Place in a large saucepan and cover with hot water. With the saucepan lid on, bring the water to a boil and continue boiling for 15 minutes. Turn off the heat and leave the jars in the hot water until just before they are to be filled. Invert the jars onto a clean kitchen cloth to dry. Sterilize the lids for 5 minutes, by boiling or according to the manufacturer's instructions. Jars should be filled and sealed while they are still hot.

Contents

Wine – the magic ingredient 6
10 things you need to know about cooking with wine 8
Soups, salads and appetizers 10
Pasta and grains 26
Fish and seafood 44
Meat and poultry 64
Vegetable dishes and pulses 106
Sauces, butters and relishes 122
Sweet things and baking 134
Index 158
Acknowledgments 160

Wine – the magic ingredient

As a wine writer, I always seem to have a couple of opened bottles in the kitchen. Wine is as natural an addition to my cooking as olive oil. I add a quick splash to the pan to make an instant sauce for steak, pour a glass into the pan when I cook a roast, use the best part of a bottle to cook a slow, flavoursome braise, or sweeten it to make a fabulous fruit dessert. There are so many different ways to use it.

Wine adds flavour, first of all. It makes an everyday dish special, whether it's a simple tomato sauce or a stew. It adds a beautifully balanced acidity to a cream sauce or, when reduced to a few intense spoonfuls, a marvellous sauce of its own. It adds depth, body and richness to a stew, an appetizing sharpness to a pasta sauce.

Certain dishes are defined by wine – Coq au Vin, obviously, Moules Marinières, Spaghetti Vongole, a Slow-cooked Ragu just wouldn't be the same without it. You couldn't make them any other way, but you can experiment with the wine you use to get different effects. Vermentino for example would be a classic wine to use for a Spaghetti Vongole (see page 39) but there's no reason why you couldn't use a Picpoul or an Albariño. You might not think of pouring red wine into a risotto but with the Beetroot Risotto on page 43 it works beautifully.

Can you add wine to a korma? You certainly can and although it's entirely non-traditional, it tastes the better for it. And if you've never cooked spaghetti in red wine (see page 28) – yes, really! – you haven't lived.

So don't be afraid of using wine in your cooking. Experiment just as you would with other ingredients in your store cupboard. It's one of the easiest and most effective ways to give your food that extra lift and really wow your family and friends!

10 things you need to know about cooking with wine

Like any other ingredient you need to understand how wine works in a dish and the best techniques for using it. Here are 10 things to remember:

1. The wine you use needs to be drinkable. By that I mean it must be clean and fresh and, obviously, not corked. It shouldn't taste like vinegar or be so old it's lost all its fruit. If you have leftover wine decant it into a smaller bottle or container so that the air doesn't get to it. Wine that's been left open for 4–5 days is probably OK. Wine that's been sitting in your cupboard for 4–5 months generally isn't.

2. That doesn't mean it has to be the wine you normally drink. I've had great success using sweeter wines such as white Grenache or blush Zinfandel which are not particularly to my taste but which are great in a recipe or cocktail (see Frosé on page 151).

3. Don't use wines labelled as cooking wines which tend to be particularly poor quality and not that much of a saving over a cheap bottle of wine.

4. On the other hand don't feel you have to use an expensive wine. The only circumstances in which I'd advocate it is if a dish needs only a small amount of wine and you'd otherwise have to open another bottle. To steal a glass from the bottle you're planning to drink may be the cheapest way to make the dish.

5. You need a less good wine if you're cooking a slow-cooked dish like a stew than if you're quickly deglazing a pan. A good trick is to add a small dash of better wine at the end of a long braise which makes it taste as if that's the wine you've cooked with.

6. The most versatile wines are crisp, dry, unoaked whites such as Pinot Grigio and medium-bodied but not overly tannic reds like Merlot. Wines with a pronounced aromatic character such as Riesling or Gewürztraminer are less flexible, but may turn out to be delicious with, for example, a creamy sauce. Feel free to experiment.

7. Fortified wines such as Sherry, Madeira and Marsala are great for cooking. A small quantity adds strength, depth and often a welcome sweetness.

8. Reducing a wine by simmering will accentuate its dominant character such as sweetness, tannin or acidity. But it's a useful way of concentrating flavour when you want to add a small amount to a dish or dressing.

9. A wine-based marinade will tenderize meat but it will change the flavour and make it more 'gamey' if you do it for longer than a couple of hours. You should also discard the marinade unless you're going to cook it well. (See the Red Wine Marinated Venison Steaks on page 98.)

10. Even in recipes that feature a significant amount of wine you usually need another ingredient such as stock, cream or passata/strained tomatoes to balance it. A homemade chicken or vegetable stock is a boon. Freeze leftover wine in an ice cube tray and keep the cubes handy in a freezer bag to add to a dish.

Finally, a question I'm often asked. If you cook with wine is there any alcohol left in the dish? There is a widespread misconception that it all cooks out but unless you're cooking the dish for 3 hours or more there will be a residue depending on how much wine you've used. Worth bearing in mind if you're cooking for kids or non-drinkers.

Soups, salads and appetizers

Red chicory, roquefort and hazelnut salad with moscatel dressing

It might not occur to you to use wine in a salad dressing but in fact it saves you from having to buy a lot of expensive flavoured wine vinegar. For this recipe you want a light Moscatel not a dark sticky one.

50 g/$^1/_3$ cup roasted, skinned hazelnuts*
2 heads of red or green chicory
2 Comice or Conference pears, peeled and cut into 8 segments
100 g/$^3/_4$ cup Roquefort, roughly crumbled

FOR THE DRESSING
2 tablespoons light sweet Moscatel or southern French Muscat, such as Muscat de St Jean de Minervois
1 tablespoon white wine vinegar
2 tablespoons mild olive oil
sea salt and freshly ground white pepper

Serves 4

Preheat the oven to 180°C (350°F) Gas 4.

Freshen up the hazelnuts by roasting them in the oven or toasting them in a dry frying pan/skillet. Set aside to cool and chop roughly.

Separate out the chicory leaves and place in a bowl of iced water for 15–20 minutes. Drain and pat the leaves dry with a kitchen towel.

Make the dressing. Measure out the sweet wine, white wine vinegar and the olive oil into a jam jar and give it a good shake. Alternatively put the ingredients in a bowl and whisk together. Adjust the amount of wine, vinegar or oil to taste – add a dash more wine if it needs the sweetness or vinegar if it needs the acidity. Season with sea salt and freshly ground white pepper, to taste.

Arrange the salad on individual plates starting with a pile of chicory leaves, then the pear segments and Roquefort. Re-whisk or shake the dressing, check the seasoning and spoon over the salad. Top with the chopped hazelnuts.

*If you can't find skinned hazelnuts roast them with their skins on until dark brown then rub off the skins with a kitchen towel.

What to drink

A lush white wine such as an oak-aged Sauvignon or Sauvignon-Semillon blend.

Smoked duck, mandarin and pecan salad with pinot noir and pomegranate dressing

Red wine can be used in place of wine vinegar to make a deliciously fruity dressing. Making a red wine reduction like this is a thrifty way to use up leftover wine, and it will keep in the refrigerator for several days.

3 mandarin oranges or other small sweet oranges
100 g/3½ oz. lamb's lettuce/mâche or watercress
225 g/8 oz. smoked duck breast, sliced
100 g/¾ cup candied pecans* or walnuts

FOR THE DRESSING
225 ml/scant 1 cup Chilean or other inexpensive Pinot Noir, or another fruity red wine
1½ tablespoons light muscovado sugar
100 ml/⅓ cup plus 1 tablespoon light olive oil
1 medium pomegranate
½–1 teaspoon pomegranate molasses or balsamic vinegar
sea salt and freshly ground black pepper

Serves 6

Peel and slice the oranges horizontally, reserving any juice. Cut the larger slices in half to make half-moon shapes.

To make the dressing, put the wine in a small saucepan, bring to the boil, then lower the heat. Simmer for 10–15 minutes or until the wine has reduced by two-thirds (leaving about 5 tablespoons). Remove the pan from the heat, stir in the muscovado sugar and let cool.

Once cool, whisk in the olive oil and season to taste with salt and pepper. Cut the pomegranate in half and scoop the seeds into a bowl, catching any juice. Discard the pith and tip the seeds and juice, along with any juice from the oranges, into the dressing. Add the pomegranate molasses or balsamic vinegar to taste. Stir well.

Divide the lamb's lettuce/mâche or watercress between six plates and arrange the duck breast and orange slices on top. Scatter over the candied pecans or walnuts. Give the dressing a quick whisk, then spoon it over the salad. Serve immediately.

* If you can't find candied pecans, put 100 g/¾ cup pecans in a dry, non-stick frying pan/skillet and sprinkle over 1 teaspoon caster/granulated sugar. Toast gently over medium heat for a couple of minutes, shaking the pan frequently, until the nuts are crisp and the sugar has caramelized.

What to drink

The dressing is quite intense, so choose an equally powerful New World Pinot Noir from, for example, California, Oregon, Chile or Central Otago in New Zealand to stand up to it.

White onion and bay leaf soup with raclette and toasted hazelnuts

I tasted this soup at one of my favourite Bristol restaurants, Wallfish, and begged the chef, Seldon Curry, for the recipe. It sounds like a lot of onions and butter – it is – but trust me it works. He used a local Somerset cheese called Ogleshield but I'm suggesting the more widely available Raclette here.

125 g/$1\frac{1}{8}$ sticks butter
1.25 kg/44 oz. white onions, finely sliced
1 teaspoon salt
2 bay leaves
3 tablespoons dry white wine
25 g/3 tablespoons plain/all-purpose flour
600 ml/$2\frac{1}{2}$ cups whole/full-fat milk, plus extra if you need it
175 g/2 cups plus 1 teaspoon grated Raclette or Ogleshield cheese

FOR THE GARNISH
3 tablespoons rapeseed oil
75 g/$\frac{1}{2}$ cup roasted hazelnuts, roughly chopped
2 tablespoons freshly chopped parsley

Serves 4–6

Melt the butter in a large pan and tip in the onions. Stir thoroughly then add the salt, bay leaves and wine. Put a lid on the pan and cook over a low heat for about 45 minutes until deliciously soft and sweet.

Sprinkle over the flour, stir and cook for 5 minutes then gradually add the milk, stirring until smooth, and continue to cook over a low heat for about 15 minutes. Remove the bay leaves, add the Raclette then take off the heat, cool and pass in batches through a blender until smooth*. You can sieve/strain it for extra smoothness if you want. Return to the pan, check the seasoning, adding a touch more milk if you need to thin it down.

To serve, ladle into warm bowls, drizzle the rapeseed oil over the soup and sprinkle over the chopped hazelnuts and parsley.

* If you only have a food processor rather than a blender I'd suggest straining the onions after you have cooked them then processing them into a purée, adding about half the reserved liquid. Sprinkle the flour into the remainder of the liquid then cook it out and add the milk as described above. Add this mixture back to the purée along with the cheese and whizz again.

What to drink

A smooth, dry white wine such as a Soave or Roero Arneis.

Summer pea and asparagus velouté

A velouté is a silky-smooth soup made with good stock and cream and a perfect vehicle for the new season's peas and asparagus. A splash of white wine makes it even more luxurious. You could make it with frozen peas but it wouldn't taste as good as they're grown for sweetness these days. Similarly it tastes much better if you use homemade stock and I'm afraid chicken is better than veggie stock in this recipe.

250-g/9-oz. bunch of asparagus
30 g/$^1/_4$ stick butter
1 small onion, finely chopped
2 tablespoons smooth dry white wine, such as white Burgundy or other subtly oaked Chardonnay
600 ml/2$^1/_2$ cups light chicken stock, preferably homemade
200 g/1$^1/_3$ cups fresh peas, podded
double/heavy cream, to serve
sea salt and freshly ground white pepper

Makes 4 small bowls

Rinse the asparagus. Break off the tough woody ends about one-third of the way up each spear and discard. Slice off the tips about half way down what remains of the spear and set aside. Finely slice the middle section of the spears and cut the tips in half or quarters depending on how thick they are. Set the tips aside.

Heat the butter in a lidded pan and tip in the onion and sliced asparagus. Season with salt, put a lid on the pan and cook over a low to medium heat for about 5 minutes until the vegetables are tender.

Add 300 ml/1$^1/_4$ cups of the stock to the pan and bring to the boil. Add the peas and cover and simmer for about 3–4 minutes until tender. You want to cook them for the shortest possible time to preserve their colour.

Strain the vegetables, keeping the cooking liquid. Put the vegetables in a blender and whizz until smooth, adding back the liquid you cooked them in and the remaining stock. Pass the soup through a sieve/strainer back into the pan. Cook the asparagus tips briefly in a steamer or microwave. Quickly heat through the soup.

Divide the asparagus spears between four warm bowls and ladle the soup on top. Add a swirl of cream to each bowl and serve immediately.

What to drink

A crisp dry white wine such as a Chablis or other white Burgundy. Other crisp dry whites such as Albariño or Greco di Tufo would also work well.

Warm scallop salad with crispy pancetta and parsnip chips

Cooking scallops is a bit like cooking a steak. You can sear them, then make a delicious dressing with a dash of wine mingled with the pan juices.

12 medium-sized fresh scallops, removed from their shells
1 tablespoon olive oil, plus extra for dressing the salad
100 g/3½ oz. pancetta cubes
4 tablespoons Chardonnay, Viognier or other full-bodied white wine
2 tablespoons fish stock or water
1 tablespoon double/heavy cream or crème fraîche
about 80 g/3 oz. mixed salad leaves
sea salt and freshly ground black pepper

FOR THE PARSNIP CRISPS
1 medium parsnip, peeled
vegetable oil, for deep-frying
sea salt

Serves 4

To make the parsnip crisps, cut off the root end of the parsnip to leave a piece about 10 cm/4 in. long and 3–4 cm/1¼–1½ in. wide at its narrowest point. Using a mandoline or a vegetable peeler, shave off very thin slices.

Fill one-quarter of a wok with vegetable oil. Heat the oil until very hot, about 190°C (375°F), or until a cube of bread turns golden in 40 seconds. Add the parsnip slices and fry in batches for about 30–60 seconds until brown and crisp. Remove the crisps with a slotted spoon, drain on paper towels and sprinkle lightly with salt.

Season the scallops on both sides with salt and pepper. Heat 1 tablespoon olive oil in a frying pan/skillet, add the pancetta cubes and fry for about 3–4 minutes, turning occasionally, until crisp. Remove from the pan with a slotted spoon, drain on paper towels, then set aside and keep warm.

Pour off the fat from the frying pan/skillet, then return the pan to the heat for about 1 minute until almost smoking. Add the scallops to the pan and cook for 2–3 minutes, depending on their thickness, turning them over halfway through. Remove them from the pan, set aside and keep them warm.

Pour the white wine into the pan and let it bubble up. Continue cooking until the wine has reduced by half. Add the fish stock or water and keep the liquid bubbling until it has reduced to just over a couple of tablespoons. Pour any juices that have accumulated under the scallops into the pan, stir in the cream or crème fraîche and season to taste with salt and pepper. Warm through for a few seconds, then remove the pan from the heat.

Divide the salad leaves between four plates, drizzle with a little olive oil and season lightly. Scatter over the pancetta cubes and the parsnip crisps. Put three scallops on each plate, spoon over the pan juices and serve immediately.

What to drink

A white Burgundy or other cool-climate Chardonnay would be delicious with this dish.

Mushroom, mustard and madeira soup

A rich, intensely delicious soup that makes a good first course for a dinner party.

75 g/3/4 stick butter, plus a little extra for frying the mushrooms
1 medium onion, finely chopped
1 large garlic clove, finely chopped
500 g/18 oz. chestnut mushrooms
2 tablespoons Madeira or Oloroso sherry
1 teaspoon dried porcini powder (optional)*
1 litre/4 cups mushroom or vegetable stock*
1 medium potato, peeled and sliced
2 teaspoons wholegrain mustard
sea salt and freshly ground black pepper
lemon juice, to taste
double/heavy cream, to serve

Serves 4–6

Heat the butter in a large saucepan or casserole and add the chopped onion and garlic. Cook over a low heat until soft.

Wipe the mushrooms clean, trim the stalks and thinly slice, reserving a good few slices for the garnish. Tip the remaining mushrooms into the butter, stir and cook for about 15 minutes until the mushrooms are brown and the liquid has all but evaporated. Stir in the Madeira or sherry and the porcini powder if using.

Add the stock, bring to the boil then add the sliced potato. Simmer until the potato is soft. Strain, reserving the liquid and blitz in a blender or food processor, gradually adding back the reserved liquid until you have a smooth soup. Return to the pan, add the mustard and reheat gently without boiling. Check the seasoning, adding salt, pepper and lemon juice to taste.

To serve, fry the reserved mushroom slices briefly in a little butter. Ladle the soup into warm bowls, top with a swirl of cream and scatter the mushroom slices over the top.

* If you use vegetable stock I'd add some dried porcini powder to the mushrooms to intensify the flavour.

What to drink

A glass of Amontillado sherry is perfect with this or you could drink a rich Chardonnay.

Luxurious cheese fondue

If you're making a dish as simple as fondue you need to use top quality cheese. Emmental and Gruyère are traditional but once you've got the hang of it you can play around with other alternatives.

425 g/7 cups finely sliced or coarsely grated cheese, with rinds removed, such as: (150 g/1¹/3 cups Gruyère or Comté, 150 g/ 1¹/3 cups Beaufort and 125 g/1 cup Emmental, or 225 g/2 cups Gruyère and 200 g/ 1²/3 cups Emmental)
2 teaspoons potato flour or corn flour/ cornstarch
1 garlic clove, halved
175 ml/³/4 cup Muscadet, or other very dry white wine
1 tablespoon kirsch (optional)
freshly ground nutmeg and black pepper
sourdough, pain de campagne or ciabatta, to serve

A cast iron fondue pan and burner

Serves 2

Toss the sliced or grated cheese with the flour. Set aside until it comes to room temperature.

Rub the inside of the pan with the cut garlic. Start off the fondue on your cooker. Pour in the wine and heat until almost boiling. Remove from the heat and tip in about one-third of the cheese. Keep breaking up the cheese with a wooden spoon using a zig-zag motion as if you were using a wire whisk. (Stirring it round and round as you do with a sauce makes it more likely that the cheese will separate from the liquid.)

Once the cheese has begun to melt return it over a very low heat, stirring continuously. Gradually add the remaining cheese until you have a smooth, thick mass (this takes about 10 minutes, less with practice). If it seems too thick add some more hot wine. Add the kirsch, if you like, and season with nutmeg and pepper.

Place over your fondue burner and serve with bite-size chunks of sourdough or country bread.

Use long fondue forks to dip the bread in, stirring the fondue to prevent it solidifying.

What to drink

A Swiss white such as Chasselas if you can get hold of it or a white wine from the Savoie region of France such as Roussette would be traditional. Otherwise any crisp, dry white, such as Muscadet, will do.

Pasta and grains

Fish and seafood

Moules marinières with muscadet

This classic bistro dish is a wonderful way to enjoy mussels. The French would generally use a basic white vin de table, but I think it tastes particularly good with Muscadet.

1 kg/2¼ lb. fresh mussels
3 tablespoons light olive oil or sunflower oil
1 medium onion, finely chopped
2 garlic cloves, finely chopped
100 ml/⅓ cup plus 1 tablespoon Muscadet or other crisp dry white wine
3 heaped tablespoons freshly chopped parsley
your choice of chips/fries, mayonnaise and crusty bread, to serve

Serves 2

Tip the mussels into a sink full of cold water and give them a good swirl. Drain off the water, fill up the sink again and swirl the mussels once more. Discard any mussels that are open. Using a small, sharp knife, remove the hairy 'beards'. Transfer the mussels to a large bowl of fresh cold water.

Heat the oil in a large saucepan or deep flameproof casserole, add the onion and cook over a low heat for 5–6 minutes until beginning to soften. Stir in the garlic, pour in the wine, then increase the heat and bring to the boil. Drain the mussels and tip them into the pan. Turn them over in the sauce, cover the pan and cook over a high heat for 3 minutes, shaking the pan occasionally. Remove the lid and check the mussels are open. If not, cover and cook for 1 minute more. Discard any mussels that haven't opened, then sprinkle over the parsley.

Serve immediately in deep bowls accompanied by chips/fries and mayonnaise (wickedly delicious) or crusty bread.

What to drink

The remaining Muscadet would go well, or use any simple, carafe-style French white.

Cioppino

Cioppino hails from San Francisco and is a rustic stew made with fresh fish and shellfish.

FOR THE STOCK
3 tablespoons olive oil
1 medium onion, finely chopped
3 garlic cloves, crushed
1 teaspoon dried oregano
2 tablespoons dry vermouth, such as Noilly Prat (optional)
175 ml/$\frac{3}{4}$ cup dry white wine such as Picpoul de Pinet or Pinot Grigio
400 g/14 oz. fresh tomatoes, skinned, deseeded and chopped
400 g/14 oz. can cherry tomatoes
500 ml/2 cups plus 2 tablespoons fish stock or a mixture of fish stock and clam juice
a few parsley stalks
1 bay leaf
Tabasco or other hot pepper sauce
sea salt and freshly ground black pepper

FOR THE STEW
450 g/16 oz. clams or mussels
1 tablespoon olive oil
30 g/$\frac{1}{4}$ stick butter
1 medium onion, sliced
2 celery stalks, trimmed and sliced
50 ml/3$\frac{1}{2}$ tablespoons dry white wine
600 g/21 oz. firm white fish such as cod cut into chunks
300 g/10$\frac{1}{2}$ oz. raw prawns/shrimp
3 tablespoons freshly chopped flat leaf parsley
sea salt and freshly ground black pepper

TO SERVE
12–16 slices day-old baguette
olive oil
2 garlic cloves, cut in half

Serves 6–8

To make the stock, heat the oil in a large saucepan add the onion and cook over a low heat for 5 minutes until beginning to soften. Add the garlic, stir and cook for 1 minute then stir in the oregano. Turn up the heat and add the vermouth, if using, and the wine. Bubble up until it's reduced by at least half then tip in the fresh tomatoes. Stir, put a lid on the pan and cook over a low heat, stirring occasionally, until the tomatoes have broken down. Add the cherry tomatoes and fish stock and bring to the boil. Add the parsley, bay leaf and season with salt, pepper and a few shakes of Tabasco. Simmer for 15–20 minutes and set aside, removing the parsley stalks and bay leaf.

Preheat the oven to 190°C (375°F) Gas 5.

Lay the sliced baguette out on a baking sheet. Drizzle both sides of the baguette with olive oil and bake for about 10–15 minutes until crisp. Set aside to cool. Soak the clams or mussels in cold water for at least 30 minutes, scrubbing and removing the 'beards' if necessary. Heat the olive oil in a large pan, add the butter and cook the onion and celery over a low heat for 5 minutes until soft. Pour in the wine, let it reduce then turn up the heat and add the clams or mussels. Cover the pan and cook for a couple of minutes until the shells open up. Take the pan off the heat and remove any clams or mussels that haven't opened. Heat the reserved tomato stock. Place the fish and the prawns/shrimp on top of the clams or mussels and pour over the hot stock. Bring back to the boil and simmer for a minute until the fish is cooked. Carefully fold in the parsley. Rub the toasted baguette with the cut garlic cloves. Serve the stew in warm bowls handing round the toasted baguette to float on top or break into the soup.

What to drink

You can drink the same white wine you use to make the stew but a dry Provencal rosé is also particularly delicious.

Chicken with chardonnay and chanterelles

This dish is perfect for a romantic dinner for two, therefore it's worth using a really good wine to make it. You need only a glass for cooking the chicken, so the rest of the bottle can be drunk with the meal.

15 g/¹/₃ cup dried chanterelles
1 tablespoon plain/all-purpose flour
2 boneless chicken breasts, about 350 g/12 oz.
2 tablespoons olive oil
35 g/2 tablespoons plus 1 teaspoon butter
4 shallots, thinly sliced
a good pinch of Spanish sweet smoked paprika (pimentòn)
150 ml/²/₃ cup top-quality New World Chardonnay or good white Burgundy
3 tablespoons double/heavy cream
2 coils dried pappardelle all'uovo or other wide-ribboned egg pasta, about 100 g/3¹/₂ oz.
freshly grated nutmeg
1 tablespoon freshly chopped parsley
sea salt and freshly ground black pepper

an ovenproof dish

Serves 2

What to drink

The rest of the bottle you used in the recipe.

Soak the chanterelles. Drain the chanterelles, reserve the soaking liquid and strain it through a fine sieve/strainer.

Preheat the oven to 200°C (400°F) Gas 6.

Put the flour in a shallow dish and season it with salt and pepper. Dip the chicken breasts into the flour and coat both sides. Heat a medium frying pan/skillet over moderate heat, add 1 tablespoon olive oil and 10 g/ 2 teaspoons butter. When the butter is foaming, add the chicken breasts skin-side down. Fry for 2¹/₂–3 minutes until the skin is brown and crisp. Turn the chicken over and lightly brown the other side for 2¹/₂–3 minutes. Transfer the chicken to an ovenproof dish and cook in the preheated oven for 15–20 minutes until cooked.

Meanwhile, discard the fat from the frying pan/skillet and wipe the pan with paper towels. Heat the remaining oil and 15 g/1 tablespoon butter in the pan, add the shallots and fry gently for 5–6 minutes or until soft. Stir in the paprika, then increase the heat to high and add the wine. When the wine has reduced by half, add 90 ml/¹/₃ cup of the reserved mushroom water. Reduce the heat and let simmer gently for 10 minutes. Strain the sauce through a fine sieve/strainer into a heatproof bowl. Return the strained sauce to the pan, add the chanterelles, cover and simmer for 10 minutes.

Remove the pan from the heat, stir in the cream and salt and pepper to taste. Return the pan to the burner and heat very gently, stirring occasionally, until the sauce thickens.

To cook the pasta, bring a large saucepan of lightly salted water to the boil, add the pasta and cook until al dente. Drain well, add the remaining butter and season with pepper and freshly grated nutmeg.

Cut each chicken breast into five or six thick diagonal slices. Divide the pasta between two warm plates, put the slices of chicken on top, then spoon over the mushroom and cream sauce. Sprinkle with chopped parsley and serve immediately.

Slow-braised lamb shanks with red wine, rosemary and garlic

The preparation and cooking of this dish can be spread over three days, which makes it the perfect dish for Sunday lunch.

6 even-sized lamb shanks, about 2 kg/4½ lbs. in total
1 large onion, thinly sliced
3 carrots, cut into thin batons
4 garlic cloves, thinly sliced
2–3 sprigs of rosemary
½ teaspoon black peppercorns
1 bottle robust red wine, 750 ml/3¼ cups, such as Shiraz, Malbec or Zinfandel, plus 75 ml/⅓ cup extra to finish
4 tablespoons olive oil
500 ml/2 cups passata/strained tomatoes
tomato ketchup, to taste
sea salt and freshly ground black pepper
creamy mashed potatoes and green/French beans, to serve

a large heavyweight plastic bag

a large lidded flameproof casserole

Serves 6

Put the lamb shanks in a large, heavyweight plastic bag. Add the onion, carrots, garlic, rosemary and peppercorns. Pour in the bottle of wine, then pull up the sides of the bag so the marinade covers the meat. Secure the top of the bag with a wire twist. Put the bag in a bowl or dish and refrigerate overnight. The next day, remove the lamb shanks from the marinade, pat them dry with paper towels and season with salt and pepper. Strain the marinade through a sieve/strainer into a large bowl and reserve the vegetables.

Preheat the oven to 170°C (325°F) Gas 3.

Heat half the oil in a large flameproof casserole, add the lamb shanks and brown them thoroughly on all sides – you may need to do this in two batches. Remove the lamb and set it aside. Add the remaining oil to the casserole, then add the reserved vegetables and fry briefly until they begin to soften. Add a few tablespoons of the marinade and let it bubble up, incorporating any caramelized juices that have stuck to the casserole. Stir in the passata/strained tomatoes and the rest of the marinade, then return the lamb shanks to the pan. Spoon the vegetables and sauce over the lamb and bring to simmering point. Cover the meat tightly with parchment paper, put the lid on the casserole and cook in the preheated oven for 1¾–2 hours until the meat is almost tender.

Remove the lid and paper and cook for a further 30 minutes. Remove the rosemary sprigs, let cool, cover and refrigerate overnight.

The next day, carefully remove any fat that has accumulated on the surface. Reheat gently on the top of the stove until the sauce comes to simmering point. If the sauce isn't thick enough, remove the lamb shanks from the pan, simmer the sauce until it thickens, then return the lamb to the pan. Add the remaining wine and simmer for a further 15 minutes. Season to taste with salt and pepper and sweeten with a little tomato ketchup, if necessary. Serve with creamy mashed potatoes and green/French beans.

What to drink

Drink a similar wine to the one you've used to make the dish. A Malbec would be perfect.

Venison sausages with red wine and rosemary gravy

This is real comfort food, poshed up for a dinner party. Rosemary works really well with red wine in a gravy. Easy to make. Everyone will love it. Win, win!

600 g/21 oz. venison sausages

FOR THE GRAVY

4 tablespoons light olive oil
20 g/1½ tablespoons butter
2 medium red onions, thinly sliced
2 garlic cloves, crushed
1 tablespoon freshly chopped rosemary leaves
1 tablespoon tomato purée/paste
1 tablespoon plain/all-purpose flour
175 ml/¾ cup full-bodied red wine
175 ml/¾ cup beef stock
sea salt and freshly ground black pepper
mashed or baked potatoes and red cabbage, to serve

Serves 4

Heat a frying pan/skillet over a moderate heat. Add 2 tablespoons of the oil, heat for 1 minute then add the butter.

Once the butter has melted tip in the onions, stir and cook over a moderate heat until they start to brown. Add the crushed garlic and rosemary, stir and cook for another minute. Add the tomato purée/paste, stir, cook for a minute and then work in the flour.

Pour in the red wine and beef stock, bring to the boil, season lightly with salt and a generous amount of freshly ground black pepper then turn the heat right down and simmer for 15 minutes. Check the seasoning and adjust to taste.

Meanwhile brown the sausages well on all sides in the remaining oil. Drain off the fat and add the sausages to the gravy. Leave over a low heat for 10 minutes or so for the sausages to absorb some of the sauce then serve with mashed or baked potatoes. Red cabbage is also delicious with this dish.

What to drink

A hearty red such as a Malbec or Shiraz.

Duck casserole with red wine, cinnamon and olives

Red wine and cinnamon are natural partners and work together brilliantly in this exotically spiced, Moorish-style casserole. I suggest you use a strong, fruity wine such as a Merlot, Carmenère or Zinfandel.

2 duck breasts
4 duck legs
3 tablespoons olive oil
1 medium onion, thinly sliced
1 celery stalk, thinly sliced
1 garlic clove, crushed
350 ml/1½ cups full-bodied fruity red wine (see recipe introduction), plus 2 tablespoons extra
250 ml/1 cup passata/strained tomatoes
2 small strips of unwaxed orange zest
1 cinnamon stick
100 g/1 cup pitted mixed olives marinated with herbs
½ teaspoon herbes de Provence or dried oregano
sea salt and freshly ground black pepper
couscous or pilaf and leafy green vegetables, to serve

an ovenproof dish

Serves 4

Preheat the oven to 200°C (400°F) Gas 6.

Trim any excess fat from all the duck pieces and prick the skin with a fork. Cut the breasts in half lengthways and season all the pieces lightly with salt and pepper. Put 1 tablespoon oil in an ovenproof dish and add the duck pieces, skin-side upwards. Roast in the preheated oven for 20 minutes, then remove from the oven and pour off the fat (keep it for roasting potatoes). Reduce the oven temperature to 150°C (300°F) Gas 2.

Meanwhile, heat the remaining oil in a flameproof casserole, add the onion and celery and fry over a low heat for 5–6 minutes or until soft. Stir in the garlic, increase the heat and pour in the red wine. Simmer for 1–2 minutes, then add the passata/strained tomatoes, orange zest, cinnamon, olives and herbs. Transfer the duck pieces to the casserole and spoon the sauce over them. Bring the sauce to a simmer, cover and transfer the casserole to the preheated oven for about 1¼ hours until the duck is tender. Spoon the sauce over the duck halfway through cooking and add a little water if the sauce seems too dry.

Take the casserole out of the oven, remove and discard the cinnamon stick and orange zest and spoon off any fat that has accumulated on the surface. Stir in 2 tablespoons red wine and season to taste with salt and pepper. Serve with couscous or a lightly spiced pilaf along with some cavolo nero or other dark leafy greens.

Note: You can also make this casserole a day ahead. To do so, cook it in the oven for just 1 hour, then let it cool, cover and refrigerate overnight. The following day, skim off any fat, then reheat it gently, adding a final dash of wine just before serving.

What to drink

Any robust southern French, Spanish, Portuguese or southern Italian red would go well with this recipe. As would a good, gutsy Zinfandel.

Coq au vin

This classic French recipe is a terrific dish for a dinner party The French would always use a local wine to make it I'd suggest a good Côtes du Rhône-Villages, a Gigondas or Lirac.

300 g/10½ oz. shallots
3 tablespoons plain/ all-purpose flour
6 large skinless, boneless chicken breasts
3 tablespoons olive oil
125 g/4½ oz. chopped streaky/ fatty bacon or pancetta cubes
2 garlic cloves, thinly sliced
50 ml/3½ tablespoons brandy
3 sprigs of thyme
1 bay leaf
1 bottle dry fruity red wine 750 ml/3¼ cups (see recipe introduction)
250 g/3½ cups small button mushrooms
15 g/1 tablespoon butter, softened (optional)
3 tablespoons freshly chopped flat leaf parsley
sea salt and freshly ground black pepper
creamy mashed potatoes or tagliatelle, to serve

Serves 6

What to drink

Drink a similar wine to that you've used to make the dish. Say, a Côtes du Rhone-Villages or a Gigondas.

Cut the shallots into even-sized pieces, leaving the small ones whole and halving or quartering the others.

Put 2 tablespoons of flour in a shallow dish and season it with salt and pepper. Dip the chicken breasts in the flour and coat both sides. Heat 2 tablespoons olive oil in a large lidded frying pan/skillet or deep flameproof casserole, add the chicken breasts and fry for 2–3 minutes on each side until lightly browned – you may have to do this in two batches.

Remove the chicken from the pan, discard the oil and wipe the pan with kitchen paper. Return the pan to the heat and pour in the remaining oil. Add the chopped bacon or pancetta cubes and the shallots and fry until lightly browned. Stir in the garlic, then return the chicken to the pan. Put the brandy in a small saucepan and heat it until almost boiling. Set it alight with a long cook's match or taper and carefully pour it over the chicken. Let the flames die down, then add the thyme and bay leaf and pour in enough wine to just cover the chicken. Bring back to simmering point, then reduce the heat, half-cover the pan and simmer very gently for 45 minutes. (If you're making this dish ahead of time, take the pan off the heat after 30 minutes, let cool and refrigerate overnight.) Add the mushrooms to the pan and cook for another 10–15 minutes. Remove the chicken from the pan, set aside and keep it warm. Using a slotted spoon, scoop the shallots, bacon pieces or pancetta cubes and mushrooms out of the pan and keep them warm. Increase the heat under the pan and let the sauce simmer until it has reduced by half. If the sauce needs thickening, mash the remaining soft butter with 1 tablespoon flour to give a smooth paste, then add it bit by bit to the sauce, whisking well after each addition, until the sauce is smooth and glossy.

Return the shallots, pancetta and mushrooms to the pan. Check the seasoning and add salt and pepper, to taste. Cut each chicken breast into four slices and arrange them on warm serving plates. Spoon a generous amount of sauce over the chicken and sprinkle with parsley. Serve with creamy mashed potatoes or tagliatelle.

Veal scallopine with marsala

This classic quick Italian dish would traditionally be made with dry (secco) Marsala but you can use sweet (dolce) Marsala if that's what you have to hand. (Add a teaspoon of sherry vinegar to correct the sweetness if you do.) You could also use medium-dry sherry. You could equally well use pork, chicken or even turkey fillets rather than veal. The key thing is to cut and beat them out thinly.

250 g/9 oz. thinly cut veal, pork or chicken fillets
1 tablespoon plain/all-purpose flour
1 tablespoon olive oil
30 g/¼ stick butter
125 g/1¾ cup button mushrooms, cleaned and thinly sliced
75 ml/⅓ cup dry Marsala or sweet Marsala with 1 teaspoon sherry vinegar
125 ml/½ cup chicken stock
½ teaspoon freshly chopped thyme
sea salt and freshly ground black pepper
your choice of pasta or sauteed potatoes and a watercress and rocket/arugula salad, to serve

Serves 2

Trim any fat off the veal and beat out thinly between a couple of sheets of baking parchment. Put the flour in a shallow dish, season with salt and pepper, and dip the veal fillets into the flour. Heat the oil, add 15 g/⅛ stick of the butter, let it foam up then tip in the sliced mushrooms.

Lightly brown then remove from the pan. Add the remaining butter and fry the veal fillets for about 2 minutes on both sides until lightly browned. Pour in the Marsala and sherry vinegar if using and bubble up then add the chicken stock and thyme and the reserved mushrooms. Cook for 3–4 minutes turning the veal and mushrooms in the sauce.

Add a little extra stock or hot water if you want to serve it with pasta (I suggest tagliatelle or fettucine). Otherwise serve with sautéed potatoes and a watercress and rocket/arugula salad.

What to drink

A slightly tricky dish as the sauce is quite rich so you don't want a wine that's too dry. Although it's not traditional I'd go for a Grenache or a GSM (Grenache, Syrah, Mourvèdre) blend.

Pepper-crusted steaks with red wine sauce

This has to be the ultimate fast-food recipe. You can make it from start to finish in 5 minutes. The red wine gives a wonderful instant sauce that takes the dish into the luxury league. After you have made this a couple of times, you'll find you won't need measurements – just pour in a dash of brandy, half a glass of red wine and a slosh of cream to finish and away you go.

1 tablespoon mixed peppercorns
1/2 teaspoon sea salt
1 teaspoon plain/all-purpose flour
2 thinly cut rump steaks, fat removed, 125–150 g/4 1/4–5 1/2 oz. each
1 tablespoon olive oil
25 g/1 1/2 tablespoons butter
2 tablespoons brandy
75 ml/1/3 cup full-bodied fruity red wine, such as Zinfandel, Merlot or Cabernet Sauvignon
3 tablespoons fresh beef or chicken stock
1 teaspoon redcurrant jelly or a few drops of balsamic vinegar (optional)
2 tablespoons crème fraîche/sour cream
rocket/arugula salad and crusty bread, garlic mash or chips/fries, to serve

Serves 2

Put the peppercorns and salt in a mortar and pound with a pestle until coarsely ground. Tip into a shallow dish and mix in the flour. Dip each steak into the pepper mixture and press the coating in lightly, turning to coat both sides.

Heat a frying pan/skillet over a medium heat and add the oil and half the butter. Once the butter has melted, add the steaks to the pan and cook for 1 1/2 minutes. Turn them over and cook for 30 seconds on the other side. Transfer the steaks to 2 warm plates.

Pour the brandy into the pan and light it carefully with a long cook's match or taper. When the flames die down, add the wine and cook for a few seconds. Add the stock and simmer for 1–2 minutes. Sweeten with a little redcurrant jelly or balsamic vinegar, if you like, then stir in the crème fraîche/sour cream.

Pour the sauce over the steaks and serve with a rocket/arugula salad and some crusty bread. If you're not in a hurry, this also goes really well with garlic mash or chips/fries.

What to drink

This is the kind of dish that will take almost any medium- to full-bodied red, such as a Merlot, a Cabernet Sauvignon or a Shiraz.

Spring lamb stew (*Navarin d'agneau*)

Lamb is often associated with hearty meals but my version of this classic French stew is perfect for spring and early summer. Like most stews it benefits from being made at least a few hours ahead, if not overnight, so allow time for the stew to cool and refrigerate it so that you can remove any excess fat.

750 g/26 oz. lamb shoulder cut into large chunks or a combination of shoulder and neck
3 tablespoons seasoned plain/all-purpose flour
5 tablespoons olive oil
20 g/1½ tablespoons butter
125 ml/½ cup dry white wine
2 medium onions, sliced (sweet onions like oignons de lezignan would be ideal)
2 garlic cloves, crushed
1 teaspoon crushed coriander seeds
2–3 medium carrots, peeled and sliced
2–3 medium turnips, scrubbed and cut into even-sized cubes
2 tomatoes, peeled, deseeded and chopped
1 bay leaf
1 sprig thyme
a handful of flat leaf parsley stalks and leaves
500 ml/2 cups plus 2 tablespoons chicken or vegetable stock
400 g/3 cups new potatoes, washed

Serves 4–5

Pat the pieces of meat dry and roll in the seasoned flour. Heat a frying pan/skillet and add 2 tablespoons of the oil, then, when the oil has heated, the butter. Fry the meat on all sides a few pieces at a time. Remove from the pan and set aside.

Deglaze the pan with the wine and pour over the meat. Wipe the pan and return to the heat. Add the remaining oil, tip in the onions, stir and leave over a low heat until soft.

Add the garlic and coriander seeds then the carrots and turnips, cover and continue to cook for another 7–8 minutes, stirring occasionally. Stir in the remaining flour, tomatoes, bay leaf, thyme, whole parsley stalks and stock and bring to the boil. Add the meat, bring back to a simmer then cover and leave on a low heat or in a low 140°C (275°F) Gas 1 oven for 1½ hours, checking occasionally.

Remove from the oven, cool and refrigate. Spoon off and discard the fat, bay leaf and parsley stalks. Reheat gently. Cook the potatoes in boiling water until almost done then add to the stew. Leave over a low heat for 10 minutes for the flavours to combine, adding an extra dash of white wine if you think it needs it. Chop the parsley leaves and fold through.

You could add blanched fresh peas and skinned broad beans along with the potatoes if you like.

What to drink

You could either drink a rich white like a Viognier or an aged red wine like a mature Bordeaux or Rioja reserva with this dish.

Red-wine marinated venison

Wine doesn't have to be used for a sauce. You can simply use it as a marinade to add flavour although this recipe offers the best of both worlds: a rich-flavoured marinade and a spoonful or two of delicious cooking juices. A quick, delicious treat of a dinner for two.

2 venison fillets, 125 g/ 4½ oz. each
150 ml/⅔ cup full-bodied red wine
a sprig of rosemary
2 garlic cloves, crushed
3 tablespoons beef or chicken stock
1 tablespoon olive oil
your choice of polenta, chips/ fries and green leafy vegetables, to serve
sea salt and freshly ground black pepper

Serves 2

Measure 100 ml/⅓ cup plus 1 tablespoon of the red wine into a flat dish, add the rosemary and the crushed cloves of garlic and turn the venison fillets in the marinade. Leave to marinate for 3–4 hours turning them once.

Heat a ridged griddle pan or a heavy-bottomed frying pan/skillet for a few minutes. Remove the venison fillets from the marinade and pat dry. Rub a little oil into them then lay them onto the hot pan and cook for about 3 minutes. Turn them carefully and cook for another minute. Set the venison aside to rest for about 5 minutes.

Remove the pan from the heat and deglaze with the remaining red wine and stock. Bubble up until reduced. Check the seasoning adding salt and pepper, to taste. Serve on warm plates with polenta or chips/fries and some cavolo nero or other dark leafy greens.

What to drink

This would show off a good red wine like a red Bordeaux or similar cabernet-merlot blend.

Osso buco-style veal chops with green olive gremolata

Osso buco is one of those dishes about which huge arguments rage. Whether there should be tomato or no tomato. Whether it should be cooked for one hour or three. Well, this version gives the dish a complete makeover. It's fresher and faster, but just as delicious.

4 large veal chops, about 1 kg/2¼ lb. in total
2 tablespoons olive oil
15 g/1 tablespoon butter
1 small onion, finely chopped
1 celery stick, thinly sliced
2 garlic cloves, crushed
150 ml/⅔ cup Italian dry white wine, such as Pinot Grigio
150 ml/1 cup passata rustica/strained tomatoes or regular passata
about 300 ml/1¼ cups light vegetable or chicken stock

FOR THE GREEN OLIVE GREMOLATA

finely grated zest of 1 lemon
10 pitted green olives, finely chopped
3 heaped tablespoons freshly chopped parsley
your choice of saffron risotto, rice or green salad, to serve

Serves 4

Trim any excess fat from the chops. Heat a large shallow frying pan/skillet and add the oil. Heat for 1 minute, then add the butter. When the foaming has subsided, add the veal chops and fry them for about 3 minutes on each side until nicely browned. Remove the chops from the pan and set aside.

Add the onion and celery to the pan and cook over a low heat for 5–6 minutes until softened. Stir in the garlic, then increase the heat to high and pour in the wine. Let it bubble up for a few minutes until the wine has reduced by half, then add the passata/strained tomatoes and 225 ml/scant 1 cup of the stock. Stir well, then return the chops to the pan, spooning the sauce over them. Bring the sauce back to a simmer, half-cover the pan and reduce the heat. Cook very gently for 30–40 minutes, turning the chops halfway through, until they are tender. If they seem to be getting dry, add a little more stock.

Meanwhile, to prepare the gremolata, put the lemon zest, chopped olives and parsley in a bowl and mix well. When the chops are ready, add half the gremolata to the pan and stir to mix. Cook over a very low heat for 5 minutes for the flavours to amalgamate.

Transfer the chops to four warm plates, spoon the sauce over the top and sprinkle with the remaining gremolata. Serve with a saffron risotto, plain boiled rice or a simple green salad.

What to drink

I'd personally drink a dry Italian white with this, such as an Orvieto or Verdicchio dei Castelli de Jesi, but you could opt for an Italian red – a Barbera, for example.

Sauces, butters and relishes

Jamon and pink peppercorn butter

I got this idea from one of my favourite local Bristol restaurants, Bell's Diner. They serve it instead of butter with the sourdough bread they offer at the beginning of the meal. It's the perfect use for offcuts from a Spanish ham on the bone. Use slightly more wine and slightly less butter if the ham is fatty.

125 g/1 cup ham offcuts from a Spanish ham bone
60 ml/¼ cup dry white wine
1 teaspoon pink peppercorns crushed with a mortar and pestle or ½ teaspoon crushed black pepper
125 g/1⅛ sticks unsalted butter at room temperature, cut into cubes
sourdough or rye bread, to serve

Enough for 6–8

Put the ham in the bowl of a food processor and blitz until it's finely chopped. Add the wine and whizz until it forms a thick paste. Add the crushed peppercorns and work in the softened butter using the pulse button.

What to drink

Fino sherry always goes well with ham but a glass of Albariño or dry rosé would be enjoyable too.

Chorizo butter

A robust, spicy butter you can melt onto a steak or a pork or lamb chop.

70 g/generous ½ cup chopped chorizo
1 garlic clove, crushed
3 tablespoons red wine
70 g/⅔ stick soft butter, cut into cubes
2 tablespoons freshly chopped parsley
freshly ground black pepper

Enough for 6–8

Put the chorizo in the bowl of a food processor. Add the crushed garlic and wine and whizz until it forms a thick paste. Add the softened butter using the pulse button. Add the parsley and season generously with black pepper.

Tip the chorizo butter onto a piece of foil and shape into a rectangle. Use the foil to roll the butter into a sausage shape, twist the ends like a Christmas cracker and chill until firm.

Remove from the refrigerator 20–30 minutes before serving. Cut into thin slices and melt onto a steak or a pork chop.

Simple lemon, cream and chive sauce

A deliciously indulgent white wine sauce with which you can anoint a simple piece of fish, jazz up a salmon-en-croute or even use as a pasta sauce for two (it's good with prawns/shrimp).

3 tablespoons dry white wine
40 g/3 tablespoons soft butter, cut into cubes
grated zest of 1/2 lemon
75 ml/1/3 cup double/heavy cream
1 heaped tablespoon freshly snipped chives
sea salt and white pepper

Serves 2

Measure the white wine into a small saucepan, heat and reduce by half. Whisk in the butter, then add the lemon zest and double/heavy cream and stir. Warm through gently, taking care not to bring the liquid to the boil, then stir in the chives.

If you use this sauce to coat fish you've just poached or microwaved, add a couple of spoonfuls of the cooking juices too.

Cheese and garlic spread

This is barely a recipe, more an ingenious way to use up the tail ends of pieces of cheese. The French call it 'fromage fort'.

250 g/9 oz. assorted bits of cheese, at room temperature
2 garlic cloves, peeled and roughly chopped
3/4 tablespoon dry white wine
1/2 teaspoon coarsely ground black pepper
2 tablespoons freshly chopped parsley

Serves 2

Sort through the cheese, removing the rind and cut into cubes. Put the garlic in a food processor and whizz until finely chopped. Add the cheese and pulse a few times then add the wine and whizz until you have a spreadable consistency. Add the black pepper and parsley and pulse to incorporate. Transfer to a bowl, cover and ideally leave in the fridge for a couple of hours for the flavours to develop. Serve on crackers or crostini.

Light chicken jus

These are two riffs on an accompaniment to roast chicken – the first a lighter, French-style sauce without flour, the second a more classically English gravy. Personally I'd have the former in summer and the latter in winter.

1 oven-ready chicken, approx. 2 kg/4½ lbs.
75 ml/⅓ cup dry white wine
200 ml/scant 1 cup chicken stock
sea salt and freshly ground black pepper
lemon juice (optional)

Serves 4

Preheat the oven to 200°C (400°F) Gas 6.

Season the bird with salt and pepper and place in a roasting pan. Put in the preheated oven for 40 minutes. Remove the bird from the oven, tip the pan and carefully pour off all but a couple of spoonfuls of pan juices. Baste the chicken with the juices and pour the white wine round the chicken and return to the oven for a further 40–50 minutes. Once the chicken is cooked set it aside to rest. Skim off any excess fat from the pan juices. Return the pan to a very low heat and work the stuck-on pan juices off the sides with a wooden spoon, adding a splash more wine if there isn't much left in the pan. Add the stock and bubble up until slightly reduced. Check the seasoning and adjust to taste. Strain through a fine-meshed sieve/strainer, if desired.

Roast chicken gravy

75 ml/⅓ cup white or red wine
20 g/2⅓ tablespoons plain/all-purpose flour
350 ml/1½ cups hot chicken or turkey stock, preferably homemade
sea salt and freshly ground black pepper
Amontillado sherry or Madeira (optional)

Serves 4–6

Follow the recipe for Light Chicken Jus up to the point where you skim off the excess fat. Sprinkle the flour into the pan and work into the pan juices. Whisk in the hot stock, bring to the boil and simmer for about 5 minutes, adding a little extra stock if it's too thick. Season with salt and pepper to taste. A dash of Amontillado sherry or Madeira can be good if you want a richer, more full-flavoured stock. If you've roasted garlic with the chicken you can pop a couple of soft cloves out of their skins and mash them into the pan for extra flavour.

Cep gravy

This is one of my favourite ways to make gravy and particularly good with roast beef.

25 g/¾ oz. dried ceps
2 tablespoons olive oil
3 banana shallots, peeled and finely sliced
20 g/1½ tablespoons butter
1 garlic clove, crushed
1 tablespoon plain/all-purpose flour
75 ml/⅓ cup red wine
roasting and/or meat juices
sea salt and freshly ground black pepper

Serves 4

Soak the ceps for at least half an hour in hand hot water to cover. Slice roughly, retaining the soaking liquid. Heat the oil in a shallow pan and add the sliced shallots. Cook over a low heat until beginning to soften. Stir in the butter then add the crushed garlic. Cook for another 5 minutes or so until the shallots start to turn golden. Add the flour, stir and cook for a minute then pour in the wine. Allow to reduce and thicken then add the ceps and their soaking liquid. Bring up to the boil then turn the heat down and simmer for 15 minutes. Once your meat is cooked and rested add any skimmed meat juices or add the gravy to the juices in the roasting pan, adding extra water if needed. Reheat and serve. You can strain the gravy if you want for a smoother texture.

Plum and pinot jam

Wine gives jam/jelly an exotic lift. I originally made this jam with windfall plums, but it was so good I make it every year now.

1 kg/2¼ lb. plums
250 g/1¼ cups preserving sugar
300 g/1½ cups granulated sugar
2 tablespoons pomegranate molasses
6–8 cardamom pods, lightly crushed
1 teaspoon ground cinnamon
50 ml/3½ tablespoons Pinot Noir
50 ml/3½ tablespoons water

sterilized glass jars (see page 4)

Serves 4

Halve the plums, twist and remove the stones/pits, then cut into two or three pieces. Place in a large saucepan or preserving pan with the sugars, pomegranate molasses, cardamom pods, cinnamon and Pinot. Place over a very low heat until the sugars have completely dissolved then bring to the boil and boil hard for about 15 minutes until the jam is set. Remove the cardamom pods, skim the jam and rest for 10 minutes, then put into hot, sterilized jars.

Fig and walnut relish

This is one of those recipes that came about by happy accident while trying to use up the Christmas leftovers. It makes the perfect accompaniment to the remains of the Stilton – or any other crumbly blue cheese.

125 g/scant 1 cup dried figs, preferably organic
50 ml/3½ tablespoons tawny port
30 g/¼ cup walnut kernels

sterilized glass jar (see page 4)

Serves 4

Snip the figs into quarters and place in a sterilized jar. Mix the port with 50 ml/3½ tablespoons of water, pour over the figs, put a lid on the jar and give it a good shake. Leave the figs to marinate for at least 24 hours. Toast the walnut pieces lightly in a dry pan and chop roughly. Cool and stir into the figs.

Apricot and moscatel relish

Wine can be used instead of vinegar to add a sharp counterpoint to the sweetness of a jam or relish. This is delicious with seared or smoked duck, grilled/broiled pork or cold ham.

2 tablespoons light olive oil or sunflower oil
1 medium white onion (about 100 g/3½ oz.), finely chopped
600 g/3⅓ cups fresh apricots, stoned/pitted and halved
25–40 g/2–3¼ tablespoons soft brown sugar
2 strips of orange peel, with as little pith as possible
4–5 cloves
4–5 tablespoons Moscatel such as Moscatel de Valencia
sea salt

sterilized glass jars (see page 4)

Serves 4

Heat the oil in a medium-sized saucepan, add the onion, stir, turn the heat down, cover and cook over a low heat for about 10 minutes until the onion is soft. Tip in the apricots, 25 g/2 tablespoons of sugar, the orange peel, cloves, a pinch of salt and 4 tablespoons Moscatel. Stir and bring to the boil, reduce the heat, cover and cook for about 20–25 minutes until the apricots are soft. Check the seasoning adding a splash more wine or sugar to taste. Remove the cloves and orange rind and transfer to sterilized jars.

Sweet things and baking

Red wine and cherry ripple ice cream

With so many ice creams available to buy, it might seem unnecessary to make your own, but this version is worth it.

6 large/US extra-large egg yolks
125 g/$^2/_3$ cup minus 2 teaspoons caster/ granulated sugar
560 ml/$2^1/_3$ cups single/light cream
2 tablespoons whole/full-fat milk
1 teaspoon pure vanilla extract

FOR THE CHERRY SAUCE
350 g/$1^3/_4$ cups pitted dark red cherries or a large jar of Morello cherries, drained
125 g/1 cup fresh or frozen raspberries
3–4 tablespoons caster/ granulated sugar
100 ml/$^1/_3$ cup plus 1 tablespoon fruity red wine, such as Merlot
1 tablespoon kirsch or cherry brandy (optional)

an ice cream maker (optional)

Serves 4–6

To make the cherry sauce, put the cherries, raspberries and 3 tablespoons caster/granulated sugar in a saucepan. Heat gently, stirring occasionally, until the sugar has dissolved. Add 75 ml/$^1/_3$ cup wine, bring to the boil and simmer for 10–15 minutes until the cherries are soft and the liquid is syrupy. Taste and add extra sugar, if necessary. Let cool, then chill in the refrigerator.

Put the egg yolks and 110 g/$^1/_2$ cup plus 1 tablespoon caster/granulated sugar in a heatproof bowl and beat with a hand-held electric mixer until smooth, pale and moussey. Put the cream, milk and remaining sugar in a saucepan and heat gently until almost boiling. Pour the hot cream over the egg mixture in a steady stream, whisking constantly until smooth.

Pour the custard through a fine-mesh sieve/strainer back into the rinsed pan. Heat very gently, stirring constantly with a wooden spoon, until the custard thickens and coats the back of the spoon. If it looks like it's starting to boil, remove the pan from the heat and stir for a couple of minutes to let cool slightly before returning it to the burner. Stir in the vanilla extract, then let the custard cool completely. Pour the cold custard into a plastic container and place it in the freezer. Remove it after about 1 hour when the edges have begun to harden. Beat with a hand-held electric mixer. Return to the freezer, then beat again after 30 minutes. (Or churn in an ice cream maker.)

When the mixture is the consistency of soft-scoop ice cream, take half the cherry sauce and cut up any larger pieces of fruit. Fold a few teaspoons of the mixture into the ice cream, turn the ice cream over with a tablespoon and repeat until half of the cherry mixture has been incorporated. Freeze the ice cream for several hours and refrigerate the rest of the sauce.

Transfer the ice cream to the refrigerator for 15–20 minutes to soften slightly before serving. Meanwhile, put the remaining cherry mixture, the remaining wine and a splash of kirsch or cherry brandy, if using, in a saucepan and heat gently until almost boiling. Let cool for 10 minutes. Serve the ice cream in scoops with the warm cherry sauce poured over.

What to drink

Wine, even sweet wine, doesn't stand up that well to ice-cream but you could try a modern super-fruity style of ruby port.

PX Tiramisu

PX stands for Pedro Ximenez – a wickedly treacly style of sherry, which of course comes from Spain, not Italy but nevertheless makes a fantastic tiramisu with a lovely raisiny flavour.

250 g/1 generous cup mascarpone
100 ml/1/3 cup plus 1 tablespoon PX sherry
3 large/US extra-large eggs
50 g/1/4 cup unrefined caster/granulated sugar
125 ml/1/2 cup strong espresso coffee
1 tablespoon brandy
16–18 Savoiardi biscuits/cookies
2–3 teaspoons unsweetened cocoa powder
a little grated dark/bittersweet chocolate, to serve

a medium-sized rectangular dish about 24 x 16 x 8 cm/ 9 1/2 x 6 1/4 x 3 1/4 in.

Serves 4–6

Tip the mascarpone into a bowl with 3 tablespoons of the PX sherry and beat with a wooden spoon until smooth.

Separate the eggs, putting the yolks into a large bowl and two of the whites into another bowl. Add the sugar and beat at high speed with electric beaters until the mixture is, pale, light and moussey. Tip half the mascarpone into the egg mixture and beat it in on medium speed then repeat with the remaining mascarpone. Wash the beaters and dry thoroughly then beat the egg whites until stiff and fold into the mascarpone. Set aside while you prepare the biscuits/cookies.

Pour the coffee into a shallow dish and add the remaining PX and brandy. Dip half the biscuits/cookies on both sides into the coffee and lay them in the dish, breaking them in half as necessary to fit. Top with half the mascarpone mixture and sift over a teaspoon of cocoa powder. Repeat with the remaining biscuits/cookies and top with the rest of the mascarpone. Sprinkle with another teaspoon of cocoa, cover the dish with clingfilm/plastic wrap and refrigerate for at least 6 hours. Remove the clingfilm/plastic wrap and grate over the dark/bittersweet chocolate before serving.

What to drink

Frankly there's more than enough booze in the dessert but you could always pour small glasses of PX!

Super-boozy Christmas fruit cake

I was given this recipe by my late mother in law when I first got married and have used it ever since. It makes the most fabulously moist cake. I prefer to top it with dried fruits rather than the usual royal icing.

225 g/1½ cups sultanas/golden raisins
225 g/1½ cups seedless (dark) raisins
350 g/2½ cups currants
50 g/⅓ cup undyed glacé/candied cherries
8–10 tablespoons medium-dry Amontillado sherry
275 g/2 cups plain/all-purpose flour
¼ teaspoon salt
½ teaspoon ground cinnamon
½ teaspoon ground nutmeg
2½ teaspoons unsweetened cocoa powder
1 teaspoon gravy browning powder (in the original but optional)
225 g/2 sticks unsalted butter at room temperature
225 g/1 cup plus 2 tablespoons caster/granulated sugar
4 eggs
50 g/½ cup chopped almonds
finely grated zest of ½ unwaxed orange
2 tablespoons apricot jam/jelly, to glaze
ready-to-eat dried fruits and nuts, to decorate

23-cm/9-in. cake pan, base and sides lined with non-stick baking parchment

Makes 18–20 slices

Measure out the dried fruits, cherries and nuts into a plastic box or large storage jar and pour over the sherry. Mix well and leave to soak for a couple of days, stirring or shaking the fruit every 12 hours or so.

Sift the flour, salt, cinnamon, nutmeg, cocoa powder and gravy browning, if using, together.

Preheat the oven to 150°C (300°F) Gas 2.

Cream the butter with the sugar until light and fluffy. Beat in the eggs, one at a time, beating well after each addition. Add a spoonful of flour after each egg to prevent curdling. Mix in all the soaked fruit, the almonds, orange zest and the remaining flour mixture and beat thoroughly.

Transfer the cake mixture into the prepared pan. Press down firmly, smooth the top with a spatula or wooden spoon and hollow out at the centre slightly. Bake for 3½ hours until firm to the touch and cooked through. Cover the cake lightly with foil after 2 hours to prevent it over-browning. When the cake it ready remove from the oven and leave in the pan for 20 minutes. Transfer the cake to a wire rack to cool completely. Remove the baking parchment and wrap in fresh greaseproof paper and foil and store in an airtight container for about a month before decorating or icing.

To decorate, briefly microwave 2 tablespoons of apricot jam/jelly and 1 tablespoon water. Sieve/strain and keep warm in a bowl over a pan of simmering water. Brush over the top of the cake. Arrange the dried fruits and nuts over the top of the cake and brush with the remaining glaze.

What to drink

This recipe already has a fair amount of booze in it but if you're feeling especially indulgent, a small glass of sweet sherry or Madeira would be the icing on the cake!

Orange syllabub with crunchy orange sprinkle

Syllabub – a velvety-smooth concoction of sweet wine and cream – is one of the great English puddings, dating from the 16th century. I like it, for a change, made with orange rather than lemon and topped with what my daughter calls 'orange sprinkle', an irresistibly crunchy mixture of orange zest and sugar.

150 ml/2/3 cup southern French Muscat or other strong sweet white wine (15 per cent ABV)
1 tablespoon Cointreau or other orange liqueur
finely grated zest of 2 unwaxed oranges
4 tablespoons caster/granulated sugar
2 tablespoons freshly squeezed orange juice
2 tablespoons freshly squeezed lemon juice
400 ml/1 3/4 cups double/heavy cream, chilled

1 large bowl, chilled for 30–40 minutes in the refrigerator

6 glass dishes

Serves 6

Pour the wine into a bowl, add the Cointreau or orange liqueur, half the grated orange zest, the orange and lemon juice and 2 tablespoons sugar. Stir, cover and refrigerate for several hours or overnight.

Mix the remaining orange zest and sugar in a bowl. Spread it over a plate and leave for a couple of hours to crisp up. Store it in an airtight container until ready to use.

Strain the wine mixture through a fine, non-metallic sieve/strainer. Pour the cream into the large chilled bowl and beat with a hand-held electric mixer until it starts to thicken. Gradually add the orange-flavoured wine, beating well after each addition until the cream thickens again – you want a thick pouring consistency. When the final addition of wine has been incorporated the mixture should hold a trail when you lift out the beaters, but it shouldn't be stiff. (Don't overbeat it, or it will separate.) Ladle the mixture into six individual glass dishes and chill them in the refrigerator for at least 1 hour before serving.

Just before serving, sprinkle the orange sugar over the top of each dish.

What to drink

I don't think you need to serve wine with this syllabub, but a small glass of well-chilled Sauternes or late-harvested or botrytized Sauvignon or Sémillon would go well.

Roasted pears with sweet wine, honey and pine nuts

Roasting pears in wine transforms them from everyday fruit into a light but luxurious dinner party dessert. Their gentle flavour makes a perfect foil for a fine dessert wine. The trick is to use an inexpensive wine for cooking and a better wine of the same type to serve with it.

freshly squeezed juice of 1 large lemon
9 medium just-ripe Conference pears
50 g/3½ tablespoons butter, softened
3 tablespoons clear fragrant honey, such as orange blossom
175 ml/¾ cup Premières Côtes de Bordeaux or a late harvested Sauvignon or Sémillon
50 g/½ cup pine nuts
2 teaspoons caster/granulated sugar
200 ml/1 scant cup double/heavy cream
2 teaspoons vanilla sugar

a large ovenproof dish, buttered (large enough to take the pears in a single layer)

Serves 6

Preheat the oven to 190°C (375°F) Gas 5.

Strain the lemon juice into a small bowl. Cut the pears in half, peel them and remove the cores. Dip the pear halves in the lemon juice (this will prevent them discolouring), then put them, cut-sides upwards, in the prepared ovenproof dish. Make sure the pears fit snugly in one layer. Put a small knob of butter in the hollow of each pear, then drizzle them with the honey, wine and any remaining lemon juice.

Bake the pears in the preheated oven for 50–60 minutes, turning the pears over halfway through. If you notice while the pears are cooking that they are producing a lot of juice, increase the oven temperature to 200°C (400°F) Gas 6 to concentrate the juices and form a syrup. Remove the pears from the oven and let cool for about 20 minutes.

Meanwhile, lightly toast the pine nuts in a dry, non-stick frying pan/skillet, shaking the pan occasionally, until they start to brown. Sprinkle over the sugar and continue to cook until the sugar melts and caramelizes. Put the cream and vanilla sugar in a small saucepan and heat gently, stirring occasionally, until lukewarm.

To serve, put three pear halves on each plate and spoon over some of their cooking syrup. Trickle over 1 tablespoon warm cream and scatter over a few caramelized pine nuts. Alternatively, serve the cream separately for your guests to pour over.

What to drink

This is a good dessert to pair with a Sauternes or another sweet Bordeaux.